Flowers, and Husbandry in Shakespeare's Plays

Pamela Milne

FLOWERS, HERBS
AND
HUSBANDRY
IN
SHAKESPEARE'S PLAYS

First Edition 2004
Published by Pamela Milne

Quotations from Shakespeare's plays
Selected by Pamela Milne

Commentary and Footnotes
Written by Pamela Milne

Photographs
Taken by Pamela Milne

Desktop Publishing by Maureen Pritchett

First Edition 2004 published by Pamela Milne
36 Waverley Park, Great Shelford, CB2 5BA UK

Consultancy and Typesetting by Maureen Pritchett
66 Gough Way, Cambridge CB3 9LN England UK

A CIP catalogue record for this book is available from the British Library.

ISBN No. 0-9548150

Printed in England 2004

CONTENTS

INTRODUCTION

Reading through Shakespeare's plays over the years, I've been utterly astonished at the great number of references concerning flowers, herbs, and what was once called husbandry but what would now be called farming or gardening. How could this most prolific writer of plays and poems, using a quill pen and relying on candlelight when daylight was finished, find time to acquire such an extensive knowledge of nature?

One has to remember that he was brought up by the banks of the river Avon in very pleasant countryside. He obviously noted and enjoyed, not only the flowers and herbs which would have bloomed in his father's garden, but also the masses of varied wild flowers of the time which would have been a sheer delight for anyone with eyes to see.

Shakespeare loved the countryside and was seriously disturbed by the possibility of war, not only for its cruel effects on men and their families, but also for the devastating results on the land and its flora and fauna.

INTRODUCTION (continued)

Who but Shakespeare, confronted by the possibility of war, would have made one of his characters profess distress at the wreckage of wild flowers trampled under the hooves of horses?

'No more the thirsty entrance of this soil
Shall daub her lips with her own children's blood;
No more shall trenching war channel her fields,
Nor bruise her flowerets with the armed hooves
Of hostile paces.'

(Henry IV Pt. 1 Act 1 Sc. 1)

I hope anyone reading this book will be surprised, like myself, at the sheer number of references to these plants and be grateful that many of the flowers and herbs enjoyed by Shakespeare are left to us today, although sadly and inevitably in far fewer numbers!

My thanks to Maureen Pritchett M.A. (Oxon) for her patience in putting the original typescript on computer and for her enthusiasm and advice re publication.

My thanks to Denis Bartlett for reading the script and for his amendments and advice.

Pamela Milne

INDEX OF FLOWERS

INDEX OF HERBS / WEEDS

INDEX OF PHOTOGRAPHS

FLOWERS

* *The photograph of Daffodils at Anglesey Abbey is printed by kind permission of the National Trust*

HERBS / WEEDS

ROSES
(Roseaceae)

Shakespeare makes more mention of roses than of any other flower. It is often used to describe the characters' emotions – they blush like a red rose, grow pale like a white rose and, of course, the rose is inevitably connected with romance!

One is not quite sure which species Shakespeare had in mind but the Dog Rose (Rosa canina) was certainly growing profusely in the countryside at that time. It was actually then know as the Dag Rose – a dag being a dagger – on account of its very sharp thorns and Shakespeare often referred to the thorns and prickles of the rose. Indeed on occasion he uses the beauty of the flower as opposed to the thorns as a simile for good versus evil.

(Henry IV Pt. 1 Act 1 Sc. 3)

Inevitably he has a field day with the Wars of the Roses in Henry VI Pts. I, II and III, showing both sides of the argument but always stressing the fearful consequences of war. The emblem of the House of York was the white Rosa alba semi-plena, and that for the House of Lancaster was the red Rosea gallica officinalis, this being the first and most famous of the gallica roses

ROSES
(Roseaceae)

ALL'S WELL THAT ENDS WELL

Diana

Ay, so you serve us
Till we serve you! But when you have our roses –
You barely leave our thorns to prick ourselves,
And mock ourselves with our bareness.
(Act 4 Sc. 2)

ANTONY AND CLEOPATRA

Cleopatra [1]

What, no more ceremony? – See, my women!
Against the blown rose may they stop their nose,
That kneel'd unto the buds.
(Act 3 Sc. 11)

HAMLET

Hamlet

Such an act,
That blurs the grace and blush of modesty,
Calls virtue, hypocrite; takes off the rose
From the fair forehead of an innocent love
And sets a blister there.
(Act 3 Sc. 4)

HENRY IV Pt. 1

Hotspur

To put down, Richard, that sweet lovely rose,
And plant this thorn, this canker, Bolingbroke?
(Act 1 Sc. 3)

---

[1] ***One can sympathise with Cleopatra - sycophants quickly change their allegiance at the fall of a star!***

Sweet Violet (Viola odorata)

Cowslips (Primula veris)

Primroses (Primula vulgaris)

Fleur-de-Luce (Iris pseudacorus)

HENRY VI Pt I

Plantagenet [1]
Let him that is a true-born gentleman,
And stands upon the honour of his birth,
If he suppose that I have pleaded truth,
From off this briar pluck a white rose with me.

Somerset
Let him that is no coward, nor no flatterer,
But dare maintain the party of the truth,
Pluck a red rose from this thorn with me.

Warwick
I love no colours; and, without all colour
Of base insinuating flattery,
I pluck this white rose with Plantagenet.

Suffolk
I pluck this red rose with young Somerset;
And say withal, I think he held the right.

Vernon
Stay lords and gentlemen; and pluck no more,
Till you conclude – that he upon whose side
The fewest roses are cropped from the tree,
Shall yield the other in the right opinion.
...

Vernon
Then for the truth and plainness of the case,
I pluck this pale and maiden blossom here,
Giving my verdict on the white rose side.

Somerset
Prick not your finger as you pluck it off;
Lest, bleeding, you do paint the white rose red.

Lawyer
Unless my study and my books be false,
The argument you held was wrong in you;
In sign whereof, I pluck a white rose too.

---

1 ***The emblem of the House of York was Rosa alba semi-plena, and for the House of Lancaster Rosa gallica officinalis, the first and most famous of the gallica roses.***

HENRY VI Pt I (continued)

Plantagenet	Now, Somerset, where is your argument?
Somerset	Here, in my scabbard; meditating that Shall die your white rose a bloody red.
Platagenet	Meantime, your cheeks do counterfeit our roses; For pale they look with fear, as witnessing The truth on our side
Somerset	No, Plantagenet, 'Tis not for fear, but anger, - that thy cheeks Blush for pure shame, to counterfeit our roses: And yet thy tongue will not confess thy error.
Plantagenet	Hath not thy rose a canker, Somerset?
Somerset	Hath not thy rose a thorn, Plantagenet? …
Somerset	Well, I'll find friends to wear my bleeding roses, That shall maintain what I have said is true, Where false Plantagenet dare not be seen. …
Plantagenet	And, by my soul, this pale and angry rose, As cognisance of my blood-drinking hate, Will I, for ever, and my faction wear.
Warwick	Against proud Somerset and William Poole, Will I upon thy party wear this rose; And here I prophesy, - this brawl today Grown to this faction, in the Temple garden, Shall send between the red rose and the white, A thousand souls to death and deadly night. (Act 2 Sc. 4)

HENRY VI Pt. 2

York	Then will I raise aloft the milk-white rose With whose sweet smell the air shall be perfum'd. (Act 1 Sc. 1)

HENRY VI Pt. 3

Richard	I cannot rest Until the white rose that I wear be dyed Even in the luke-warm blood of Henry's heart. (Act 1 Sc. 2)
King Henry	Woe upon woe! Grief more than common grief! ...
(to a father who has killed his son in battle) [2]	The red rose and the white are on his face, The fatal colours of our striving houses: The one, his purple blood right well resembles; The other, his pale cheeks, methinks, present: Wither one rose and let the other flourish! (Act 2 Sc. 5)

LOVE'S LABOUR'S LOST

Biron [3]	At Christmas I no more desire a rose, Than wish a snow in May's new-fangled shows. (Act 1 Sc. 1)
Prince	Will they return?
Boyet	They will, they will, God knows, And leap for joy, though they are lame with blows: Therefore change favours, and when they repair, Blow like sweet roses in this summer air.
Prince	How blow? How blow? Speak to be understood.
Boyet [4]	Fair ladies mask'd, are roses in their bud: Dismask'd, their damask sweet commixture shown, Are angels vailing clouds or roses blown. (Act 5 Sc. 2)

---

[2] Shakespeare was so clearly aware of the horrendous results of war.

[3] An example of Shakespeare's awareness of the rightness of seasons.

[4] To vail – to avail, to cause to fall down, the clouds open as the angels descend.

MERRY WIVES OF WINDSOR

Hugh

In shallow rivers, to whose falls
Melodious birds sing madrigals,
There will we make our beds of roses,
And a thousand fragrant posies.
(Act 3 Sc. 1)

A MIDSUMMER NIGHT'S DREAM

Lysander

Why is your cheek so pale?
How chance the roses there do fade so fast?
(Act 1 Sc. 1)

Titania [5]

The seasons alter: hoary-headed frosts
Fall in the fresh lap of the crimson rose;
And on old Hymen's chin, and icy crown,
An odorous chaplet of sweet summer buds
Is, as in mockery, set:
(Act 2 Sc. 2)

Thisbe [6]

Most radiant Pryamus, most lily-white of hue
Of colour like the red rose on triumphant briar.

Titania [7]

Come sit down upon this flowery bed,
While thy amiable cheeks do coy,
And stick musk-roses in thy sleek smooth head,
And kiss thy fair large ears, my gentle joy.
(Act 4 Sc. 1)

---

[5] ***Hymen – the God of Marriage.***

[6] ***The briar was the sweet briar (once known as eglantine) which produced a beautiful scent from the leaves (Rosa rubiginosa).***

[7] ***The musk-rose was an old-fashioned rose grown chiefly for its strong scent.***

OTHELLO

Othello

When I have plucked the rose,
I cannot give it vital growth again,
It needs must wither: I'll smell thee on the tree.
(Act 5 Sc. 2)

RICHARD II

Queen [8]

But soft, but see, or rather do not see,
My fair rose wither: yet look up; behold;
That you may in pity dissolve to dew …
(Act 5 Sc. 1)

RICHARD III

Tyrrell

"O thus", quoth Dighton, "lay the gentle babes", -
"Thus, thus", quoth Forrest, "girdling one another
Within their alabaster innocent arms:
Their lips were four red roses on a stalk …"
(Act 4 Sc. 3)

ROMEO AND JULIET

Juliet [9]

That which we call a rose
By any other name would smell as sweet
So Romeo would, were he not Romeo called,
Retain that dear perfection which he owns
Without that title.
(Act 2 Sc. 2)

Friar

The roses in thy cheeks and lips shall fade
To pearly ashes.
(Act 4 Sc. 1)

---

[8] ***Richard's sad queen watching her husband on his way to the Tower.***
[9] ***Surely the quotation most often thought of in connection with the rose.***

TAMING OF THE SHREW

Petruchio

Say that she frown:
… I'll say she looks as clear
As morning roses newly washed with dew.
(Act 2 Sc. 1)

TWELFTH NIGHT

Duke [10]

For women are as roses; whose fair flower,
Being once display'd doth fall that very hour.
(Act 2 Sc. 4)

Olivia

Cesario, by the roses of the spring,
By maidhood, honour, truth and everything,
I love thee so that, maugre all my pride,
Nor wit nor reason can my passion hide.
(Act 3 Sc. 1)

TWO GENTLEMAN OF VERONA

Julia

The air hath starved the roses in her cheeks,
And pinch'd the lily-tincture of her face.
(Act 4 Sc. 4)

[10] ***Not a very kind observation of women!***

LILIES
(Lilaceae)

Lilies are mainly used in the Plays to imply purity and innocence. For this reason one thinks of the Madonna Lily (Lilium candidum). Christians dedicated this to the church as a symbol of purity.

According to the apothecary, Gerard, famous also as a botanist and gardener, 'Our English white lily groweth in most gardens of England.'

Gerard, wearing his apothecary's hat, also says 'The root of the garden lily stamped with honey gleweth together sinews that be cut asunder. It bringeth the hairs again upon places which have burned or scalded, if it be mingled with oil or grease …'

The Crown Imperial Lily (Fritillaria imperalis) is also mentioned. [11]

(A Winter's Tale, Act 4 Sc. 3).

A very striking plant but of no medicinal value.

---

[11] ***See Perdita's speech in the Miscellaneous section on page 41.***

LILIES (Lilaceae)

CYMBELINE

Iachimo

Cytherea, how bravely thou becom'st thy bed!
Fresh lily! And whiter than the sheets.
(Act 2 Sc. 2)

HENRY VIII

Cranmer (speaking of Princess Elizabeth)

She must die … yet a virgin,
A most unspotted lily shall she pass
To the ground, and all the world shall mourn her.
(Act 5 Sc. 4)

KING JOHN

Constance (speaking of Arthur)

But thou art fair; and at thy birth, dear boy,
Nature and fortune joined to make thee great;
Of nature's gifts thou mayst with lilies boast,
And with the half-blown rose.
(Act 3 Sc. 1)

Salisbury [12]

Therefore to be possessed with double pomp,
To guard a title that was rich before;
To gild refined gold, to paint the lily,
To throw a perfume on the violet …
(Act 4 Sc. 2)

MIDSUMMER NIGHT'S DREAM

Thisbe

Asleep, my love? What, dead, my dove?
O Pyramus, arise,
Speak, speak. Quite dumb? Dead, dead? A tomb
Must cover thy sweet eyes;
These lily lips, this cherry nose,
These yellow cowslip cheeks,
Are gone, are gone: lovers, make moan!
His eyes were green as leeks.
(Act 5 Sc. 1)

---

[12] ***A description of unnecessary adding to perfection!***

TITUS ANDRONICUS

Marcus Andronicus Oh had the monster seen those lily hands
Tremble like aspen leaves upon a lute;
And make the silken strings delight to kiss them,
He would not then have touched them for his life.
(Act 2. Sc. 4)

TITUS ANDRONICUS

Titus Andronicus Thy husband he is dead; and for his death
Thy brothers are condemn'd, and dead by this.
Look, Marcus! Ah, son Lucius, look on her!
When I did name her brothers, then fresh tears
Stood on her cheeks, as doth the honey-dew
Upon a gather'd lily almost withered.
(Act 3 Sc. 1)

TROILUS AND CRESSIDA

Troilus [13] O, be thou my Charon,
And give me swift transportance to those fields
Where I may wallow in the lilybeds
Proposed for the deserver.
(Act 3 Sc. 2)

TWO GENTLEMEN OF VERONA

Launce Now, Sir, this staff is my sister; for, look you,
She is as white as a lily and as small as a wand.
(Act 2 Sc. 3)

---

[13] ***This is surely a reference to the White Asphodel, a member of the Lily family, connected with the Elysian Fields – the home of the dead in Greek mythology, rowed there by Charon.***

SWEET VIOLETS
(Viola odorata)

The violet ranks high in the number of Shakespearean references, and there are many illusions to its perfume, which means that the sweet violet must have been the species he had in mind. Here there are no thorns, no prickles, no 'reverse side of the coin', and one gets the feeling that Shakespeare was truly fond of this small flower.

In Mrs. Grieve's Herbal (1931), she says ' the violet is very abundant in Stratford-upon-Avon', adding that 'violets, mentioned by Homer and Virgil, were used by the Athenians to moderate anger and procure sleep'.

There is also an association with death – Ophelia mentions this in Hamlet (Act 4 Sc. 5), and I think it's possible that the connection of violets with the mourning colour of purple goes back to Shakespearian times.

The Romans were known to have made wine from violets, and this must surely mean that the ancient meadows and bridle paths must have been strewn with wild flowers both then and also in Elizabethan times.

Early Purple Orchid (Orchis mascula)

Crowflower (Ragged Robin) (Lychnis folscuculi)

Corncockle (Agrostemma githago)

Daffodils/Narcissus (Narcissus pseudonarcissus)

VIOLETS
(Viola Odorata)

CYMBELINE

Queen

So, so; well done, well done:
The violets, cowslips and the primroses,
Bear to my closet: Fare thee well, Pisanio.
Think on my words.
(Act 1 Sc. 6)

Belarius

O thou goddess,
Thou divine nature, how thyself thou blazon'd
In these two princely boys! They are gentle
As zephyrs, blowing below the violet,
Not wagging his sweet head: and yet as rough,
Their royal blood enchaf'd, as the rud'st wind,
That by the top doth take the mountain pine
And make him stoop to the vale.
(Act 4 Sc. 2)

HAMLET

Ophelia

There's a daisy:
I would give you some violets,
But they withered all when my father died:
They say, he made a good end.
(Act 4 Sc. 5)

Laertes [1]

Lay her i' the earth
And from her fair and unpolluted flesh
May violets spring.
(Act 5 Sc. 1)

---

[1] ***Examples of the violet being used as a symbol of death – maybe the idea of purple as a colour of mourning springs from medieval times.***

HENRY V

King Henry [2]

I think the king is but a man as I am,
The violet smells to him as it doth to me.
(Act 4 Sc. 1)

KING JOHN

Salisbury

To throw a perfume on the violet,
To smooth the ice, or add another hue
Unto the rainbow, or with taper-light
To seek the beauteous eye of heaven to garnish,
Is wasteful and ridiculous excess.
(Act 4 Sc. 2)

MEASURE FOR MEASURE

Angelo

The tempter or the tempted, who sins most?
Not she; nor doth she tempt; but it is I,
That lying by the violet, in the sun,
Do, as the carrion does, not as the flower,
Corrupt with virtuous season.
(Act 2 Sc.2)

PERICLES

Marina

No: I will rob Tellus of her weed,
To strew thy green with flowers: the yellows, blues,
The purple violets, and marigolds,
Shall as a carpet hang upon thy grave,
While summer days do last.
(Act 4 Sc. 1)

---

[2] ***Rather enchanting that Shakespeare used the humble violet as a sign of equality between royalty and the common man.***

RICHARD II

Duchess [3] Welcome my son: who are the violets now
That strew the lap of the new-come spring?

Aumerie Madam, I know not, nor I greatly care not;
God knows I had as lief be none, as one.

York Well, bear you well in this new spring of time,
Lest you be cropped before you come to prime.
(Act 5 Sc. 2)

TWELFTH NIGHT

Duke If music be the food of love; play on,
Give me excess of it; that, surfeiting,
The appetite may sicken and so die.
That strain again; - it had a dying fall;
O, it came o'er my ear like the sweet sound
That breathes upon a bank of violets,
Stealing, and giving odour.
(Act 1 Sc. 1)

A WINTER'S TALE

Perdita [4] … violets, dim,
But sweeter than the lids of Juno's eyes,
Or Cytherea's breath.
(Act 4 Sc. 3)

---

[3] A somewhat curious reference to the violet which in this context seems to imply 'Who are the up-and-coming men?'

[4] More of Perdita's speech is quoted in the Miscellaneous section on page 41.

COWSLIPS (Primula veris)

The cowslip has many country names, such as the Key Flower, owing to its resemblance to a bunch of keys, namely the Keys of the Kingdom supposed to have been dropped by St. Peter.

Long ago women used an ointment made from cowslips as an aid to the complexion. Culpeper said 'Our city dames know well enough that the ointment or the distilled water of it adds to beauty or at least restores it when lost. It taketh away spots and wrinkles of the skin'. This is referred to in 'A Midsummer Night's Dream' (Act 2 Sc. 1) when The Fairy talks of 'Rubies, fairy favours, in those freckles live their savours'.

Another herbalist, Turner, puts the same idea thus: 'Some women, we find, sprinkle ye floures of cowslip with white wine and after wash their faces with that water to drive wrinkles away and to make them fayre in the eyes of the worlde rather than in the eyes of God, Whom they are not afrayd to offend'.

Of course, cowslip wine was at one time very popular but these flowers being now a protected species, it is no longer made. This must be one of the reasons why cowslips are making a comeback in the countryside.

COWSLIPS (Primula veris)

CYMBELINE

Iachimo [5] … On her left breast
A mole cinque-spotted, like the crimson drops
I' the bottom of a cowslip.
(Act 2 Sc. 2)

A MIDSUMMER NIGHT'S DREAM

Fairy [6] And I serve the fairy queen,
To dew her orbs upon the green:
The cowslips tall her pensioners be;
In their gold coats spots you see;
Those be rubies, fairy favours,
In their freckles live their savours:
(Act 2 Sc. 1)

THE TEMPEST

Ariel (Song) Where the bee sucks, there suck I;
In a cowslip's bell I lie:
…
Merrily, merrily, shall I live now
Under the blossom that hangs on the bough.
(Act 5 Sc. 1)

---

[5] The 'crimson drops' and 'rubies' refer to red spots on the cowslip petals – not so much in evidence now but maybe today's plants are a different strain.
[6] Orbs are the old name for fairy rings.
Pensioners were the name for Queen Elizabeth's handsome male attendants!
The favours referred to were the cowslip's supposed aid to the complexion. (see foreword on cowslips)

PRIMROSES
(Primula vulgaris)

Although not of the rose family, the name primrose comes from prima rosa – first rose, presumably as it blooms in the spring long before one can hope to see roses in flower.

The most well known quotations from the Plays come from 'The primrose path'(Hamlet, Act 1 Sc.3) and the 'Primrose way' (Macbeth, Act 2 Sc. 1).

As, by today's standards, these references mean something like 'On the road to ruin', this seems a rather curious use of the innocent-looking primrose!

Shakespeare sometimes referred to 'Pale primroses' and once in 'A Midsummer Night's Dream' and once in the poem 'Venus and Adonis', his character lay on a primrose bank – "Witness this primrose bank whereon I lie!" - maybe as a young man Shakespeare disported himself on such a bank!

In olden times tea was sometimes made from primroses, and this was supposed to have a calming effect on hysteria. Maybe in today's hectic world, this should be marketed for general consumption!

PRIMROSES
(Primula vulgaris)

CYMBELINE

Arviragus[7]

With fairest flowers,
Whilst summer lasts, and I live here, Fidele,
I'll sweeten thy sad grave: thou shalt not lack
The flower that's like thy face, pale primrose; nor
The azur'd harebell, like thy veins; no, nor
The leaf of eglantine, whom not to slander,
Outsweeten'd not thy breath:
(Act 4 Sc. 2)

HAMLET

Ophelia[8]

But, good my brother,
Do not, as some ungracious pastors do,
Show me the steep and thorny way to heaven;
Whilst like a puffed and reckless libertine
Himself the primrose path of dalliance treads,
And recks not his own read.
(Act 1 Sc. 3)

HENRY VI Pt II

Queen Margaret

And for myself, foe as he was to me,
Might liquid tears, or heart offending groans,
Or blood-consuming sighs recall his life;
I would be blind with weeping, sick with groans,
Look pale as primroses with blood-drinking sighs,
And all to have the noble duke alive.
(Act 3 Sc. 2)

---

[7] ***The eglantine was an old name for the sweet briar, known for the sweet scent of its leaves.***

[8] ***Cf. the 'Primrose path' in Hamlet and the 'Primrose way' in Macbeth.***

MACBETH

Porter [9]

Here's a knocking indeed! If a man were porter of
Hell-gate, he should have old turning the key.
Knock, knock, knock! Who's there,
I' the name of Beelzebub? Here's a farmer
That hanged himself on the expectation of plenty;
Come in time; have napkins enow about you;
Here you'll sweat for't.
...
Knock, knock, knock! Who's there!
Faith, here's an English tailor come hither,
For stealing out of a French hose;
Come in, tailor; here you may roast your goose.
Knock, knock: never at quiet. What are you?
But this place is too cold for hell.
I'll devil-porter it no further:
I had thought to let in some of all professions
That go the primrose way to the everlasting bonfire.
Anon, anon! I pray you, remember the porter.
(Act 2 Sc. 1)

A MIDSUMMER NIGHT'S DREAM

Hermia

And in the wood, where often you and I
Upon faint primrose beds were wont to lie,
Emptying our bosoms of their counsel sweet,
There my Lysander and myself shall meet;
(Act 1 Sc. 1)

A WINTER'S TALE

Perdita

… pale primroses
That die unmarried, ere they can behold
Bright Phoebus in his strength, a malady
Most incident to maids.
(Act 4 Sc. 3)

---

[9] Cf. the 'Primrose path' in Hamlet and the 'Primrose way' in Macbeth.

Poppies (Papaver somniferum)

Eryngo (Sea Holly) (Eryngium maritimum)

Thyme (Thymus serpyllum)

Fennel (Foeniculum vulgare)

MISCELLANEOUS

CYMBELINE

Musicians [1] SONG

Hark! Hark! The lark at heaven's gate sings,
And Phoebus 'gins arise,
His steeds to water at those springs
On chalic'd flowers that lies;

And winking Mary-buds begin
To ope their golden eyes;
With everything that pretty is;
My lady sweet, arise;

Arise, arise!

(Act 2 Sc. 3)

HAMLET

Ophelia [2] There's rosemary, that's for remembrance;
Pray, love, remember:
And there is pansies, that's for thoughts.

Laertes A document in madness;
Thoughts and remembrance fitted.

(Act 4 Sc. 5)

---

[1] Mary-buds – an old name for marigolds which were dedicated to the Virgin Mary and used to decorate churches with flowers.

[2] Rosemary – at one time considered to have the power to strengthen the memory.

Pansies – named from the French 'Penser' to think.

HAMLET (continued)

Ophelia [3]

There's fennel for you, and columbines –
There's rue for you; and here's some for me:
We may call it herb-grace of Sundays:
O, you must wear your rue with a difference.
There's a daisy: (Act 4 Sc. 5)

Queen [4]

There is a willow grows aslant a brook,
That shows his hoar leaves in the glassy stream;
There, with fantastic garlands did she come,
Of crow-flowers, nettles, daisies and long purples,
That liberal shepherds give a grosser name,
But our cold maids do dead men's fingers call them.
(Act 4 Sc. 7)

---

[3] Fennel – Curiously, this was once thought of as an aid to cure bad eyesight. Longfellow wrote:

"Above the lower plants it towers,
The Fennel with its yellow flowers:
And in an earlier age than ours
Was gifted with the wondrous powers
Lost vision to restore".

Rue – a very well known herb for medicinal uses. The name comes from the Greek word 'Reue' (to set free) because of the herb's effectiveness in different diseases.

[4] Crow-flower – an old name for Ragged Robin. Long Purples – the Early Purple Orchid which has tubers somewhat resembling male genitalia in shape – so inevitably used in olden times as an aphrodisiac!

LOVE'S LABOUR'S LOST

Spring Song [5]

When daisies pied, and violets blue,
And lady-smocks all silver white,
And cuckoo buds of yellow hue,
Do paint the meadows with delight…
(Act 5 Sc. 2)

MERRY WIVES OF WINDSOR

Falstaff [6]

Let the sky rain potatoes, … hail
Kissing comfits, and snow eringoes; let there come
A tempest of provocation.
(Act 5 Sc. 5)

A MIDSUMMER NIGHT'S DREAM

Oberon [7]

Yet mark'd I where the bolt of Cupid fell:
It fell upon a little western flower, -
Before, milk-white; now, purple with love's wound, -
And maidens call it love-in-idleness.
(Act 2 Sc. 2)

---

[5] ***The Cuckoo Flower is also known as Lady's Smock as the smocks worn by country lasses in olden times were often the same pale mauve colour as the flower.***

[6] ***Kissing comfits were another name for eryngoes (Eryngo maritimum), a handsome spiny plant known commonly as Sea Holly often seen on coastal shingle. In Elizabethan times the roots were sweetened with sugar and used as an aphrodisiac, hence their fascination for Falstaff!***

[7] ***Love-in-idleness is an old name for Heartsease, the wild Pansy very much connected with romance.***

A MIDSUMMER NIGHT'S DREAM (continued)

Oberon [8]

I know a bank where the wild thyme blows,
Where oxlips and the nodding violet grows;
Quite over-canopied with luscious woodbine,
With sweet musk-roses and with eglantine.
(Act 2 Sc. 2)

Titania

Fairies, be gone, and be all ways away.
So doth the woodbine the sweet honeysuckle
Gently entwist; the female ivy so
Enrings the barky fingers of the elm.
(Act 4 Sc. 1)

MUCH ADO ABOUT NOTHING

Hero

I and Ursula walk in the orchard …
Say that thou overheardest us; and bid her steal
Into the pleached bower,
Where honeysuckles, ripened by the sun,
Forbid the sun to enter.
(Act 3 Sc. 1)

A WINTER'S TALE

Autolycus [9]

When daffodils begin to peer,
With heigh! The doxy over the dale,
Why then comes in the sweet o' the year
For the red blood reigns in the winter's pale.
(Act 4 Sc. 2)

---

[8] ***Woodbine is another name for the Honeysuckle – maybe Shakespeare was thinking of two different types of honeysuckle?***
Musk-rose – a fragrant rambling rose with white flowers.
[9] ***Pale – boundary between the early and late spring.***

A WINTER'S TALE (continued)

Perdita [10]

Sir, the year growing ancient, -
Not yet on summer's death, nor on the birth
Of trembling winter, -
The fairest flowers o' the season
Are our carnations, and streak'd gilly'vors,
Which some call nature's bastards: of that kind
Our rustic garden's barren, and I care not
To get slips of them.
…

Perdita [11]

Now my fairest friend,
I would I had some flowers of the spring that might
Become your time of day; and yours, and yours,
That wear upon your virgin branches yet
Your maidenheads growing; O, Proserpina,
For the flowers now, that, frighted, thou lett'st fall
From Dis's wagon! Daffodils
That come before the swallow dares, and take
The winds of March with beauty; violets, dim,
But sweeter than the lids of Juno's eyes,
Or Cytherea's breath; pale primroses,
That die unmarried, ere they can behold
Bright Phoebus in his strength, a malady
Most incident to maids; bold oxlips, and
The crown-imperial; lilies; lilies of all kinds,
The flower-de-luce being one! O! these I lack
To make you garlands of.
(Act 4 Sc. 3)

---

[10] ***Gilly'vors – wallflowers.***

[11] ***Flower-de-luce – another name for Iris pseudacorus, not that this is a member of the Lily family! Louis VII of France originally incorporated three irises in his banner, 'Luce' being a later corruption of Louis.***

II - HERBS / WEEDS

There has always been a keen interest in herbs and their healing properties, and today that interest seems to be increasing year by year.

In Shakespeare's time herbs were of prime importance as they were used in such a diversity of ways, certainly for medical purposes, but were also kept in houses as additives to cooking, for their clean and pungent aromas, and especially for strewing on floors to offset the bad smells of discarded litter.

Elizabethan houses of any size would all have had a herb garden and their 'Simples' carefully cultivated.

Shakespeare clearly had an extensive knowledge of herbs, and also of the weeds found in the gardens and thc cornfields.

He seemed to be particularly intrigued by opiates such as the mandrake, mentioned more than once, and deemed to be Juliet's sleep-producing drink.

HERBS / WEEDS

ALL'S WELL THAT ENDS WELL

Countess	It was the death of the most virtuous gentlewoman That ever nature had praise for creating: …
Lafeu	'Twas a good lady: we may pick a thousand salads Ere we light on such another herb.
Clown [1]	Indeed, Sir, she was the sweet marjoram of the salad, Or rather, the herb-of-grace.
Lafeu	They are not salad-herbs, you knave, They are nose- herbs.

(Act 4 Sc. 5)

ANTONY AND CLEOPATRA

Cleopatra	Give me to drink mandragora.
Charmian	Why, madam?
Cleopatra [2]	That I might sleep out the great gap of time my Antony is away.

(Act 1 Sc. 5)

---

[1] Herb – of Grace – another name for Rue.

[2] Mandrake, or Mandragora, found in Mediterranean countries. Many legends attached, such as it is supposed to scream if pulled up and the up-rooter to suffer an early death. Once used as an anaesthetic during operations – the patient bit on the root.

AS YOU LIKE IT

Rosalind — O, how full of briars is this working-day world!

Celia [3] — They are but burs, cousin, thrown upon thee in
Holiday foolery; if we walk not the trodden paths
Our very petticoats will catch them.

Rosalind — I could shake them off my coat:
These burs are in my heart.
(Act 1 Sc. 3)

HAMLET

Ghost [4] — Sleeping within mine orchard,
My custom always in the afternoon,
Upon my secure hour thy uncle stole,
With juice of cursed hebenon in a vial,
And in the porches of mine ear did pour
the leprous distillment.
(Act 1 Sc. 5)

HENRY IV Pt I

Falstaff [5] — … for though the chamomile,
The more it is trodden the faster it grows,
Yet youth, the more it is wasted the sooner it wears.
(Act 2 Sc. 4)

---

[3] ***Burdock – To this day leaves its hooked bristles on clothes and dogs' fur.***

[4] ***Hebenon – considered by many to be Henbane, a truly poisonous plant. Clearly well known in Shakespeare's time, Marlowe had previously referred to 'Juice of hebon', a deadly poison.***

[5] ***Chamomile – still used as a herbal tea, said to aid the digestion. Once used as a herb for strewing the floors as it reveals a strong aroma if walked on.***

KING LEAR

Cordelia [6] (refers to Lear) [7]	Crown'd with rank fumiter, and furrow weeds, With burdock, hemlock, nettles, cuckoo-flowers, Darnel, and all the idle weeds that grow In our sustaining corn. (Act 4 Sc. 4)
Edgar[8]	Halfway down hangs one that gathers samphire, Dreadful trade! (Act 4 Sc. 6)

LOVE'S LABOUR'S LOST

Biron [9]	Sow'd cockle reap'd no corn, And justice always whirls in equal measure. (Act 4 Sc. 3)

A MIDSUMMER NIGHT'S DREAM

Bottom [10]	Good master Mustard-seed,

---

[6] Fumiter – Fumitory, a herb once used as a blood purifier.
[7] Hemlock – A very poisonous plant reputed to have caused the death of Socrates.
Darnel – A grass weed seen in cornfields.
[8] Samphire – Sometimes known as 'Poor man's asparagus'. This grew high on the cliffs of Dover, and was obviously dangerous for those trying to pick it. It now grows freely on the East Anglian coast.
[9] Corncockle – The pretty, pink-flowered corncockle used to be seen amid the corn stubble, but now, alas, very rarely.
[10] Mustard-seed – Roast beef and mustard was clearly enjoyed by Shakespeare!

A MIDSUMMER NIGHT'S DREAM) (continued)

Bottom	I know your patience well; That same cowardly giant-like ox-beef hath devoured Many a gentleman of your house: I promise you, Your kindred hath made my eyes water ere now. (Act 3 Sc. 1)
Oberon [11] (touching Titania's eyes with a herb)	Be thou as thou wast wont to be, See, as thou wast wont to see: Dian's bud o'er Cupid's flower Hath such force and blessed power. (Act 4 Sc. 1)

OTHELLO

Iago [12]	Virtue? A fig! 'tis in ourselves that we are thus, or thus. Our bodies are our gardens, to which our wills are gardeners: So that if we will plant nettles, or sow lettuce; set hyssop, And weed up thyme; supply it with one gender of herbs, or Distract it with many; either to have it sterile with idleness Or manured with industry; why, the power and corrigible Authority of this lies in our wills. (Act 1 Sc. 3)
Iago	Look, where he comes! Not poppy, nor mandragora, Nor all the drowsy syrups of the world, Shall ever medicine thee to that sweet sleep Which thou ow'dst yesterday. (Act 3 Sc. 3)

---

[11] Dian's bud – This was probably Artemesia absinthium (Wormwood). Artemesia comes from Artemis, the Greek name for Diana. This herb, once used as a mental restorative, gives the liqueur, absinthe, its name.

[12] Hyssop – once used for the cleansing of holy places. Its aromatic scent used in the perfume industry. Also in the making of chartreuse.

Rock Samphire (Crithmum maritimum)

Fungi

Hoary Plantain (Plantago media)

Mandrake (Atropa mandragora)

ROMEO AND JULIET

Benvolio [1]	Take thou some new infection to the eye And the rank poison of the old will die.
Romeo	Your plantain leaf is excellent for that. (Act 1 Sc. 2)
Friar	I must up-fill this osier cage of ours, With baleful weeds, and precious-juiced flowers. ... O mickle is the powerful grace, that lies In herbs, plants, stones, and their true qualities: For nought so vile that on the earth doth live, But to the earth some special good doth give; ... Within the infant rind of this small flower Poison hath residence, and medicine power: For this, being smelt, with that part cheers each part; Being tasted, slays all senses with the heart: Two such opposed kings encamp them still In man as well as herbs, - grace and rude will; And where the worser is predominant, Full soon the canker death eats up that plant. (Act 2 Sc. 3)
Friar	Take thou this phial, being then in bed, And this distilled liquor drink thou off: When, presently, through all thy veins shall run A cold and drowsy humour; (Act 4 Sc. 1)
Juliet [2]	What if it be a poison, which the friar

1 Plantain – an old medicinal plant, contains mucilage.

2 Juliet's sleeping drug is considered to be that of Atropa Mandragora, which is often referred to by Shakespeare as possessing strong opiate qualities.

ROMEO AND JULIET (continued)

Juliet
Subtly have minister'd to have me dead;
Alack, alack! It is not like, that I,
So early waking, - what with loathsome smells;
And shrieks like mandrakes torn out of the earth,
That living mortals, hearing them, run mad.
(Act 4 Sc. 3)

THE TEMPEST

Gonzales — Had I a plantation of this isle, my lord, -
Antonio — He'd sow it with nettle seed.
Sebastian [3] — Or docks or mallows.
(Act 2 Sc. 1)

Iris
Ceres, most bounteous lady, thy rich leas
Of wheat, rye, barley, vetches, oats and pease;
Thy turfy mountains where live nibbling sheep;
And flat meads thatch'd with stover, them to keep;
(Act 4 Sc. 1)

Prospero
… you demi-puppets that
By moonshine do the green sour ringlets make,
Whereof the ewe not bites; and you, whose pastime
Is to make the midnight–mushrooms; that rejoice to
Hear the solemn curfew;
(Act 5 Sc. 1)

---

[3] ***Mallow was often known as the bread-and-cheese plant, as children used to pick out the seeds, which tasted like cheese, and put them in their sandwiches on the way to school. Also eases wasp stings by rubbing the leaves on the affected skin. Docks have always been known to ease inflammation from nettle stings.***

A WINTER'S TALE

Perdita [4] Reverend sirs, For you there's rosemary and rue;
These keep seeming, and savour, all the winter long
Perdita [5] … Here's flowers for you;
Hot lavender, mints, savory, marjoram;
The marigold, that goes to bed with the sun,
And with him rises weeping; these are flowers
Of middle summer.
(Act 4 Sc. 3)

---

[4] Rosemary, once thought to be effective in aiding the memory, hence an emblem for lovers, Anne of Cleves, the fourth wife of Henry VIII, wore some in her hair at her wedding.
[5] Hot lavender – a certain amount of oil from this plant is dissipated by hot sun, which means that the lavender is most highly perfumed at mid-day. To avoid this dissipation of oil, the plant is best harvested early morning or evening.
Mint has been an esteemed plant for centuries. The herbalist, Gerard, says "the smelle rejoiceth the heart of man, for which cause they used to strew it in chambers and places of recreation, pleasure, repose, where feasts and banquets are made". Referred to in Chaucer and certainly grown in medieval gardens.
Savory and marjoram – plants that have been used for culinary purposes for centuries.
The marigold closes its petals at dusk and opens them in early morning.

III - HUSBANDRY

Shakespeare was clearly both interested and knowledgeable about the husbandry required for farming, and for making the Elizabethan garden a pleasure to look at.

He describes pruning, grafting, manuring and weeding – I think anyone who enjoys their Shakespeare will readily call to mind the 'dangling apricocks' in Richard II which required tying up!

There are graphic descriptions of the land that through war (Henry V Act 5 Sc. 2) or flood (Midsummer Night's Dream Act 2 Sc. 2) had been neglected until it resulted in an utter wilderness.

Shakespeare hated to see the countryside left in ruins in such a way, but with the endless wars, either against foreign countries, or civil wars such as the Wars of the Roses, men were drawn into the fighting and there was no-one left to look after the land.

HUSBANDRY

HAMLET

Hamlet

How weary, stale, flat and unprofitable,
Seem to me all the uses of this world!
Fye on't! O fye! 'tis an unweeded garden
That grows to seed; things rank and gross in nature
Possess it merely.
(Act 1 Sc. 2)

Hamlet

Repent what's past: avoid what is to come:
And do not spread the compost oe'r the weeds
To make them rank.
(Act 3 Sc. 4)

HENRY IV Pt. 2

Bardolph [1]

Live so in hope, as in early spring
We see the appearing buds; which to prove fruit,
Hope gives not so much warrant, as despair
That frosts will bite them.
(Act 1 Sc. 3)

HENRY V

Burgundy [2]

Should not, in this best garden of the world,
Our fertile France put up her lovely visage?

Alas! She hath from France too long been chased;
And all her husbandry doth lie in heaps;
Corrupting in its own fertility.

---

[1] ***Nothing changes for the aspiring gardener!***
[2] ***Shakespeare clearly abhorred the rotting, decayed state of the land as a result of war.***

HENRY V (continued)

Burgundy [3]

Her vine, the merry cheerer of the heart,
Unpruned dies: her hedges even-pleach'd,
Like prisoners wildly overgrown with hair
Put forth disordered twigs; her fallow leas
The darnel, hemlock and rank fumitory,
Doth root upon; while that the coulter rusts,
That should deracinate such savagery:

The even mead, that erst brought sweetly forth
The freckled cowslip, burnet and green clover,
Wanting the scythe, all uncorrected, rank,
Conceives by idleness; and nothing teems
But hateful docks, rough thistles, kecksies, burs,
Losing both beauty and utility.
(Act 5 Sc. 2)

HENRY VI Pt. 2

Suffolk [4]

Thy mother took into her blameful bed
Some stern untutor'd churl. And noble stock
Was graft with crab-tree slip; whose fruit thou art,
And never of the Nevils' noble race.
(Act 3 Sc. 2)

---

[3] Coulter – an iron blade in a plough.
Burnet – Mrs. Grieve's Herbal states "In the herb gardens of olden days, Salad Burnet always had its place. Bacon recommends it to be set in alleys together with the wild thyme and water mint to perfume the air".
Kecksies – these are the woody hollow stems of differing plants such as Alexanders or Hemlock.
[4] That new strains of plants can be created by grafting was clearly understood by Shakespeare.

HENRY VI Pt. 3

Richard

Revoke that doom of mercy, for 'tis Clifford;
Who not contented that he lopp'd the branch
In hewing Rutland when his leaves put forth,
But set his murthering knife unto the root
From whence that tender spray did sweetly spring.
(Act 2 Sc. 6)

HENRY VIII

Wolsey [5]

This is the state of man; today he puts forth the
Tender leaves of hopes, tomorrow blossoms …
The third day comes a frost, a killing frost,
And, - when he thinks, good easy man, full surely
His greatness is a ripening, - nips his root,
And then he falls as I do.
(Act 3 Sc. 2)

A MIDSUMMER NIGHT'S DREAM

Titania
(to Oberon)

These are the forgeries of jealousy:
And never, since the middle summer's spring,
Met we on hill, in dale, forest, or mead,
By paved fountain, or by rushy brook,
Or on the beached margent of the sea,
To dance our ringlets to the whistling wind,
Therefore, the winds, piping to us in vain,
As in revenge, have suck'd up from the sea
Contagious fogs; which, falling in the land,
Have every pelting river made so proud,
That they have overborne their continents:
The ox hath therefore stretched his yoke in vain,
The ploughman lost his sweat; and the green corn
Hath rotted, ere his youth attain'd a beard:

---

[5] ***Shakespeare so often makes the simile between the works of nature and the fate of man.***

A MIDSUMMER NIGHT'S DREAM (continued)

Titania [6] (to Oberon)	The fold stands empty in the drowned field, The crows are fatted with the murrain flock; The nine men's morris is fill'd up with mud; And the quaint mazes in the wanton green, For lack of tread, are undistinguishable. (Act 2 Sc. 2)

PERICLES

Dionyza [7]	O my distressed lord, ev'n such our griefs are; Here they're but felt, and seen with mischief's eyes, But like to groves, being topp'd they higher rise. (Act 1 Sc. 4)

RICHARD II

Gaunt [8]	And thy unkindness be like crooked age, To crop at once a too-long withered flower. (Act 2 Sc. 1)
Queen	But stay, here come the gardeners: Let's step into the shadows of these trees... (Act 3 Sc. 4)

---

[6] ***The shepherds cut lines on the turf and arranged stones which could be moved rather like a modern game of draughts – this was called nine mens' morris. This is a marvellous description of what happens to the land in time of flood.***

[7] ***This might refer to the problem of today's leylandii!***

[8] ***Dead-heading employed then as now.***

RICHARD II (continued)

Gardener [9]

Go, bind thou up yon dangling apricocks,
Which, like unruly children, make their sire
Stoop with oppression of their prodigal weight:
Give some supportance to the bending twigs.

Go thou, and like an executioner,
Cut off the heads of too-fast-growing sprays,
That look too lofty in our commonwealth:

All must be even in our government.
You thus employ'd, I will go root away
The noisome weeds, that without profit suck
The soil's fertility from wholesome flowers.

1 Servant [10]

Why should we, the compass of a pale,
Keep law, and form, and due proportion,
Showing, as in a model, our firm estate?

When our sea-walled garden, the whole land,
Is full of weeds; her fairest flowers chok'd up,
Her fruit trees all unprun'd, her hedges ruin'd,
Her knots disorder'd, and her wholesome herbs
Swarming with caterpillars?

Gardener [11]

… And Bolingbroke hath seized the wasteful king.
Oh! What pity is it,
That he had not so trimm'd and dress'd his land,
As we this garden! We at time of year

---

[9] ***A vivid description of the necessity of training fruit-trees, pruning and weeding.***
[10] ***An impressive account of a garden neglected and allowed to run wild.***
[11] ***Again, a simile showing the effects of bad husbandry and bad kingship.***

RICHARD II (continued)

Do wound the bark, the skin of our fruit-trees;
Lest, being over-proud with sap and blood,
With too much riches it confound itself;
Had he done so to great and growing men,
They might have lived to learn and he to taste,
Their fruits of duty. Superfluous branches
We lop away, that bearing boughs may live:
Had he done so, himself had borne the crown.
Which waste and idle hours hath quite thrown down.
(Act 3 Sc. 4)

RICHARD III

Queen Elizabeth	Edward, my lord, thy son is dead, Why grow the branches when the root is gone? Why wither not the leaves that want their sap? (Act 2 Sc. 2)
Buckingham	The noble isle doth want her proper limbs; Her face defac'd with scars of infamy, Her royal stock graft with ignoble plant, And almost shoulder'd in the swallowing gulf Of dark forgetfulness and deep oblivion. (Act 3 Sc. 7)

ROMEO AND JULIET

Montague (speaking of Romeo)	So far from sounding a discovery, As is the bud bit with an envious worm, Ere he can spread his sweet leaves to the air, Or dedicate his beauty to the sun. (Act 1 Sc. 1)

Extra copies of this book may be ordered from
Pamela Milne, 36 Waverley Park, Great Shelford, CB2 5BA UK
http://www.cambridgetelenet.co.uk/shakespearegarden/index.html

Flowers, Herbs and Husbandry in Shakespeare's Plays

P.S.
Quotations from Shakespeare's plays selected by Pamela Milne
Commentary, footnotes and photographs by Pamela Milne

Desktop Publishing by Rent A Temp 2004
66 Cambridge Telenet, Cambridge CB3 9LN   United Kingdom
Tel: (01223) 579100 / 508440
Contact Mrs. Maureen Pritchett M.A. (Oxon)
Email rentatemp@cambridgetelenet.co.uk
http://phonemail.co.uk/hotdesk/